Every

Single

One of You

Living Above

Single Life Frustrations

DR. DEMETRIA
SPRINGFIELD BANKS

TABLE OF CONTENTS

FOREWORD

Many who know my story, single for 44 years before God blessed me with my Prince Charming, have approached me about writing a book for singles, or requested that I conduct seminars dealing with being a Christian single. "How did you deal with being single for so long?," I am asked. "What did you do to help you through the hard times?"

Some I have talked to admit that it's a struggle for them and that the struggle is so intense at times that even they question their salvation. Others feel alone in their struggle with no one to turn to for fear that they will be frowned upon for not being able to be "happy with Jesus alone."

Still others believe that singles are treated like "odd balls" in Christian circles, believing that many programs, services and outings offered by the church mainly cater to those who are married. "Second class citizens" is how many of them feel in a place where they are told that "everybody is somebody." Thus some question their self-worth at times. Author Tyler O'Neil writes,

In churches that emphasize the importance of marriage and a culture that constantly highlights the joys of sex, single Christians struggle with questions of self worth and unfulfilled desired.

He goes on to say, however, the Bible provides them with great comfort. Indeed, the Bible has scriptures that not only comfort those who struggle with living single, but who struggle in life period.

As I already mentioned, the Lord blessed me with 44 beautiful years of being single before sending the mate He had in mind for me. Although many days felt everything except "beautiful," when I look over those years in retrospect I can truly say that they were beautiful for they have shaped me into the strong, confident, knowledgeable, selective, and persistent person I am today. With that in mind, I will also say that "It pays to wait on God!" What He does, He does well! Waiting on Him and on His divine timing, has brought to me my "Boaz" who complements me in so many ways!

The title of many of today's seminars and writing literature for Christian singles is about being "single, saved, and satisfied." Yet there are many singles today that are saved, yet unsatisfied. The struggles of the single life have been challenging and overwhelming for them to say the least. Yes, they love Jesus. Yes, some are Holy-ghost filled. Still, the single life has been an arena of much frustration, embarrassment, shame, regret, disappointment, heartbreak and heartache. "What's wrong with me?" is the question some ask themselves many days.

There are some who think that if they can get "a little more Jesus," then their struggles won't be so bad. Others think that if God would only send them the spouse that they have been praying about for so long, then EVERYTHING would be alright. Then some are just down right angry with God for "holding out" on them. While others unfortunately, have been so frustrated and disappointed that they have turned to ungodly activities – promiscuous behaviors, addictions, looking for love in all the wrong places, to name a few - all because they have felt that God has been cruel to them and cheated them out of the married life.

Is there a point of satisfaction where singles can truly be *single, saved and satisfied*, you may ask? Is there a point where a single individual – male or female will never have to deal with the frustrations of being single again? Is there truly a point of "resting in the Lord," while waiting on Him to send you the mate you have long desired?

In *Every Single One of You, Living Above Single Life Frustrations,* I will address these questions and many more. I will also share my experiences as being a single Christian – the ups the downs, the in's and the out's and how God helped me to achieve the peace, consolation and strength I so desperately needed to help me face single life struggles. With so many books available on being single and finding true contentment as a single Christian, it is my sincere prayer that "this book" satisfies the questions and longings that you have like none other; that it lifts your soul above every frustration you're experiencing, and propels you into the destiny God has for you!

Chapter One

When Are You Going to Get Married?

Alright, come on singles. We know this. The question you get asked over and over and over again is...... yep, you got it, "When are you going to get married?" A question that you sometimes want to respond to by saying at the top of your lungs, "I don't know!" I can't tell you the number of times I was asked this question and I can't tell you the number of times I said to myself "Really?" It blew my mind that other "Christians" would ask this question knowing as I did that as believers our future, our lives are in God's hand. Only He would truly know the answer. Sometimes I just wanted to say, "I want to know too!" Now I can sit back and laugh at myself.

Usually I would give the typical response (with a little cute, fake smile) and say, "When the Lord says so." Or I would shrug my shoulders and politely say, "I don't know." Or better yet I would give the politically correct answer and say, "I'm waiting on God," when I really wanted to say, "I don't know. I'm tired of waiting!" Indeed, at that moment you are gripped with many thoughts and feelings – ranging from wondering why you were asked the question in the first place since only God knows to wishing you could tell them a wedding date.

Often times the individual who asks this question is not trying to be mean or nasty or rub salt in your "wound." It's quite the contrary. What they are really saying is that to them you're a good person whose head is on straight. You deserve to have someone good in your life and it's puzzling to them that you haven't found the right person yet (in the case of a male) or the right person hasn't found you yet (in the case of a female).

As innocent as this question is, it has the potential to illicit undesirable thoughts and feelings within, further adding to the frustration and discontentment that you already feel. At first, you were "managing," but after being asked "the big question," it seems as if everything begins exploding within you as your mind becomes bombarded with questions and statements such as, "Yeah. When am I going to get married?" "Why am I still not married?" "Everyone is getting married, but me." "I must not be good enough." Or, "If I looked better, or had a better physique I would probably be married by now." What an untruth! Because if it were true? Then the attractive and shapely people that you know would all be married! However, regardless to their fancy clothes, fine cars, nice physiques and other admirable physical attributes, they too are flying solo, just like you!

What's my advice to you? Do not take this question offensively or personally. What you want to do here is rather than go home and relive the moment you were asked this question, and rather than allow your mind to dwell on negative self-talk about your single state, choose instead to think of it in the way I mentioned earlier – that you're such a hot catch that even others want to know when you are going to get married. That because you're so special that God is waiting for the right time to bless you with your mate. That He is still preparing you and your future mate to be the best for one another! Thoughts such as these not only sound better, but will make you feel a lot better.

Any thoughts contrary to these will certainly rob you of life's joy and peace. Plus, there's our enemy, the devil, who works 24/24 against the self-esteem and self-confidence of those who are single and waiting. I call him the "relentless tormenter," because he never gives up until he's robbed you of living your life to the fullest. The Bible says in John 10:10 that he comes to steal, kill and destroy. You better believe that he wants to steal, kill and destroy your joy as a single. He wants to torment you day in and day out with that innocent question "When are you going to get married?" He wants you to believe that your life would be so much better if you were married; that you could even serve God better if you were married.

I remember thinking the same things. I reasoned that if I were married I could really serve the Lord with all my heart, body, mind and soul because if I were married I would not have to deal with the yearnings of my flesh that seemed at times too much to bear. Neither would I have to deal with the tormenting thoughts of being single. Being married, I would say, would guarantee that I would have someone on my arms for every outing, movie date, Christmas and other social gatherings. However, I suspect that if I surveyed some married couples, they would say that this is not true. Some have spouses who refuse to go out with them. While, others have spouses who are too involved with their work, their friends, their careers and do not have the time to go out with them.

The truth of the matter is if you are not happy as a single, then being married won't guarantee you happiness. Let me repeat this. If you are not happy as a single individual, then becoming married won't guarantee you happiness. Why? Because you will find that marriage is not the answer to all life's problem. It is great to have a partner for life, but at the same time having a partner for life will not eliminate problems from your life.

Moreover, know that God can use you just like you are and He can give you the best life as a single! There is absolutely nowhere in the Bible where God says you are disqualified for His service because you are single! Can you imagine standing before God and He says to you "Sister _____, or Brother _____ I can't use you. You are too single for me." Or "I can't use you. You need to wait until you get married!" I'm sure that even made you laugh!

Looking back on my single days, God truly was good to me! I was able to complete two degrees beyond the bachelor's level. I traveled whenever and wherever I desired. I could pray out loud at home whenever I wanted to without someone telling me to "Be quiet!" (Lol!) I had all the time in the world to read, study and meditate on God's word, giving me a strong foundation to stand on. I enjoyed outings with my friends and family without having to worry about the demands of a family. I remember one Wednesday deciding that I wanted to go visit my cousin in Detroit. By Friday, I was long gone! See, I couldn't have taken this spur of the moment trip if I were married and had children.

Don't get me wrong. I surely HAD my share of ups and downs when I was single. Sometimes I was downright angry with God. Other times I was angry with myself for making unnecessary mistakes. Then sometimes I think I was just angry and didn't know why. But when I reflect on my time as a single, I must say being single certainly had its privileges! So stop looking at your single state through the eyes of self-pity and contempt. Stop thinking the world is against you because you are single. Even if they are, remember that if God is for you

He is more than those who are against you (Romans 8:31). All I am saying here is trust God above your single aches and pains. Trusting Him will not eliminate your pains completely, but it will help soothe you in your places of hurt. So that the next time when you are asked the infamous question "When are you going to get married?," you don't crawl in a corner thinking that something is wrong with you for not being married or crying wishing you were married. The fact that God hasn't given you a husband or wife at this point in your life doesn't mean He doesn't love you. It means that He does because He knows what is best for you.

Reflection

1. How do you feel when asked, "When are you going to get married?"

   Do you think they are intentionally trying to hurt you?

2. In your opinion, what are the benefits of being single? Purpose to re-read this list each time frustrations come.

3. Which benefits are you taking advantage of?

4. Which benefits do you want to take advantage of, but have procrastinated about?

5. How can you begin taking advantage of those benefits? Remember there's no time like the present! Ephesians 5:16 tells us to make the most of every opportunity.

Chapter Two

Hollywood, Hollywood

I believe Hollywood plays a role in the frustration experienced by some singles. Movies, especially romantic comedies, usually center on the single man or woman meeting the person of their dreams who is very well off, attractive, devoted, loving and willing to go through great lengths to win the love of the one whom they have set their sight on. What's the impact on the individual who is single? Besides drawing more attention to what they do not have (a mate), it can lure them into a world of fantasy, thinking that their rich, attractive Prince Charming or beautiful Cinderella will come along and sweep them off their feet even if they have to move the world just to do so. However, in reality we know that this is not what normally happens (more about this later).

Not to mention the fact that the majority of movies encourage sex outside of marriage as a means of expression between individuals who are "in love." Couples "living together" without holy matrimony are also portrayed as the norm. This can add additional frustration and pressure for the single Christian who is strongly admonished to live by their biblical convictions amidst a world in which "everybody is doing it."

Moreover, the coupled life is portrayed as the happy life that everyone should have, particularly around the holiday season. Here we are bombarded with love stories of couples sharing romantic holidays together; couples attending holiday functions together; couples going to great lengths to find that perfect gift for that special someone in their life. It's as if to say that if there is any time for an individual not to be single, the holidays are surely that time! There is hardly ever a movie plot where a person enjoys being single around the holidays. They must find someone! They must! Even when some of the movie plots involve singles, they are either depicted as 1) successful because they are ME-focused, focusing on getting all they can or canning all that they can get even at the expense of others (which is against God's command to be Christ-focused) or 2) frantically, desperately searching for "Mr. Right" or "Ms. Right" because in spite of their success they are lonely, unfulfilled, not having that special someone to share life with. Again, rarely is there a movie plot involving a single individual who is content in their single state.

Thus, you must protect yourself. You must protect yourself against the improper messages the media gives to the single Christian. Something you truly can accomplish! The romantic stories we see on television are primarily fictional, which means they are not true stories. The couples who meet in the movies are shown in the end as living "happily ever after;" however, the other side of the after – tests, trials and struggles are not shown.

In spite of Hollywood's focus, asking God to help you be content in your single state as you wait on His purpose to be revealed in your life will do much to help keep you level headed here. The Apostle Paul, in Philippians 4:11, wrote....*for I have learned, in whatsoever state I am, therewith to be content.* Contentment even for the Apostle Paul was a <u>learning</u> process, which means he didn't get it together over night. It is a process that will involve you making the decision to be satisfied with what God has blessed you with and where He has blessed you to be at present. Keep in mind that contentment will not eliminate your desires. You can be content as a single and still desire to get married. But, contentment will help you better cope with your desires as you wait on God's perfect timing.

Lori Smith in her article *Single Truths for Single Christians* writes,

> The extent to which we're able to be content being single depends really on what we believe about marriage.... Do we believe we're missing out? If you think that your married friends are better off, that God has overlooked you, you'll be miserable. If on the other hand, you know you're right where God wants you to be, that being unattached isn't a badge of shame, your emotions will be transformed.....What do you really believe about being single?

Our belief systems and thoughts processes affect everything in our life! That's why it is critical to have our thoughts and beliefs in line, not with our emotions, passions or feelings, but in line with the word of God!

The psalmist says *Thy word is a lamp unto my feet and a light unto my path* (Psalm 119:105). The word, not His feelings, was his gage, his measuring rod, his roadmap for life.

Although I enjoyed watching romantic comedies, particularly around Christmas time, I learned to guard my thoughts and longings when watching this type movie so that I could "keep my head above water" so to speak. I came to the point (after sulking in the house many holidays wishing that it were me in those movies) of realizing 1) that being content during the holidays and throughout the year for that matter was a matter of my choice and focus – choosing to focus on the goodness of God and what I could do to help others rather than bemoaning my single state brought strength to me in so many ways; 2) That just because I didn't have someone to share my life with at that time, didn't mean I would be single for the rest of my life; and 3) accepting the movies for what they were, nice entertainment not my life story. When feelings of self-pity would come, I would immediately cast them down; knowing that to do so was in my very best interest. Second Corinthians 10:5 says, *Casting down imagination and every high thought against the knowledge of Christ; bringing into captivity every thought to the obedience of Christ.* Lets' face it. When has dwelling on anything negative, worked for our good? Right, never.

To help you survive the media's messages that are clearly against biblical principles, you too must continually remind yourself of these things as well. You must also remind yourself of everything God has invested in you, your strengths, your positive attributes and everything else, knowing that you are something valuable even being single! Come on you can do it! You can do all things through Christ which strengtheneth you (Philippians 4:13). And trust me; Christ can strengthen you if you allow Him.

Reflection

1. After watching a movie, have you ever found yourself daydreaming about your knight in shining armor or dream girl? What effect did this have on you?

2. Have the movies ever made you feel like you were missing out because you're single? In what way(s)?

What can you do to help you in this area?

3. Are you sometimes ashamed to attend functions, particularly around the holidays because you don't have anyone to take you?

   What are some things that you can start doing to help you in this area?

4. How do you view yourself as a Christian single? Someone to be pitied? Someone to be celebrated? Someone who God has cheated out of the married life? The way you view yourself plays an important role in helping you cope with frustrations you feel.

Chapter Three

Unrealistic Expectations:
Real Life –vs- Fantasy

Another source of single life frustrations are unrealistic expectations. As I pointed out in the previous chapter, the movies can have an impact here. Again, the plot of many of Hollywood's movies depict two good-hearted people, nice looking, nice teeth (lol!), good careers and successful in search of someone special to share life with. Sometimes it's a love story where the handsome, rich Prince Charming meets the woman of his dreams who happens to be very poor. Regardless to what others are telling him, he falls in love her and the woman ends up in a position where she will never ever have to work again! Needless to say, I don't have to tell you the impact this can have on a single. It can cause them to covet this type of life. "Why can't it be you?" you ask, after all your God can do anything. So you come to the conclusion that the person you will marry should be nice looking (just like in the movies), rich (just like in the movies), drive a top of the line car (just like in the movies), and willing to do anything to have you (just like in the movies). By the way, have you ever noticed how the people in the movies can take off from work whenever they want to, for however long they wish just to go find the love of their life without ever having to worry about how their bills will get paid? Boy, fantasy, fantasy!

Frustrations are experienced by some singles because they have unrealistic expectations about what an ideal partner should be and what marriage is. In the real world, most people we meet do not make a six figure income nor are millionaires like in the movies. They are not the CEOs of companies or first level executives in the company. In the real world, many are not tall, dark and handsome or pretty and shapely with long hair. They are not the "Billy D's," "Brad Pitt's," "Denzel Washington's," "Halle Berry's" or "Julia Roberts." Some are not the best looking individuals that you ever meet. They may have a few crooked teeth or missing strands of hair.

Now don't get me wrong here. There is nothing wrong with you wanting someone that is "easy on your eyes" (Don't you just love my sense of humor!), has a good job and has a reasonable amount of intelligence. As a matter of fact, if those of us who are married would all be true here, we wanted someone that we were physically attracted to. We wanted a good provider. And, we wanted someone with some good common sense. I remember telling my mom one day that "Mom, I'm not so much focused on him having a degree as I am with him having plain old common sense." However, to compare someone you meet with the "flawless" standards or the "Hollywood pretty" that you see in the movies is not being fair to them nor is it being fair to you. Let's face it. None of us are perfect. None! Maybe he or she does not have a MBA, does that make him or her any less of a person? Perhaps their car is not the latest. But, is this really a good reason to scratch them off your list? Neither should you unrealistically expect marriage life to be the answer to all your single woes. This will only set you up for more disappointment and frustration.

To help calm your single life frustrations in this area, keep in mind that you are not going to meet "Mr. Perfect" or "Ms. Perfect." The individuals you will meet will have character flaws. They will have weaknesses. They will not be perfect in their looks. You won't like everything about them, and they will not like everything about you. To completely check them off your list because they don't measure up to everything on your checklist, again is UNREALISTIC! I'm not saying that you can't have an attractive mate or a mate that you're attracted to (because God certainly blessed me here), but be reasonable. Be realistic.

I encourage you to let go of any unrealistic expectations that you may have – about your idea mate, about marriage. The Bible is our guide for everything. Trust me, you want a mate as the Bible describes as being after God's own heart (1 Samuel 13:14.) Anything less, will spell more frustrations for you. Unrealistic expectations can cause you to end up with someone who is selfish, abusive (physically, mentally or both) and demeaning. They can also cause you to disregard the very person that God has sent your way.

Unrealistic expectations are just what the name implies – UNREALISTIC, and they can be a basis of much single life frustrations as you undergo an endless search for the person who can never measure up. No, you don't want to settle for any junk (that's another chapter by itself) and neither do you have to. Either way - setting the bar too high or too low can mean more discontentment for you.

REFLECTION

1. Do you have a list of unrealistic expectations when it comes to a potential mate or marriage? If so, what are some of them?

2. Do you possess the qualities that you desire in a mate? For example, you want them to have a MBA degree. Do you have a MBA or master's degree as well? If not, do you think it's fair to ask someone else to have something that you yourself do not?

3. What impact can unrealistic expectations have on your chances of getting the one God has for you?

4. Are you more focused on meeting a man or woman that meets all the criteria on your list or a man or woman who's after God's own heart?

I encourage you to watch Tyler Perry's movie *Temptation: Confession of a Marriage Counselor.* It will help you to reconsider your perspective on an "ideal" man or woman.

Chapter 4

I Do Mind Waiting

Sometimes you feel that if God is such a righteous God then why does He withhold that "good thing" you have been praying about. On top of that, your biological clock is ticking away. To make matters worse, your phone continues to ring informing you of old friends who have gotten married, while you're still alone. Yes you - the one who has been faithful to God; the one who shares a closeness with Him; the one who is striving to live for Him all that you know how, is still alone. It doesn't seem fair at all. "Does it really take all of this waiting?" you sometimes ask.

Prophetess Juanita Bynum sings a song entitled, *I Don't Mind Waiting*. You may be familiar with it. In it she says, *I don't mind waiting; I don't mind waiting; I don't mind waiting on the Lord. I don't mind waiting; I don't mind waiting; I don't mind waiting on the Lord.* Well another source of single life frustrations for the single is waiting! While the song says *I don't mind waiting*, many singles inwardly are singing *I do mind waiting. I'm tired of waiting on the Lord!*

Not that they don't truly love the Lord, but the waiting day after day, month after month, year after year and still coming up empty handed has wreaked havoc on their psyches! Moreover, many are coping with the fact that their biological clocks have ticked past society's ideal age for getting married. I remember saying to myself that I would marry around 25 years old and then have children around 28. Well 25 came; then 30; then 35; then 40; then 44! Little did I know the time that I would get married would be far past the age of 25! Perhaps your biological clock has ticked past your 40's or 50's. Instead of pushing the "panic button," push harder on the "prayer button." It is your focus on your age rather than on the One who is the Rock of Ages that is causing you to become weary while you wait. I guarantee you that if you take your focus off your age and replace it with thoughts of faith; you'll find yourself at more ease, peace, and contentment. Try it!

What helped me to survive frustrations in the area of waiting is that in my heart I knew that regardless to my age that if it was

God's will for me to marry, then regardless to how old I was it would most certainly come to pass! It didn't bother me that reports were saying that with so many black men being behind prison walls, this left the single black woman with little to no hope at all. Neither did it didn't bother me that statistics reported that there were 1.8 million more black women than black men. The Bible even says in Isaiah 4:1, *And in that day seven women shall take hold of one man saying, We will eat our own bread, and wear our own apparel; only let us be called by thy name, to take away our reproach.* "I'm willing to share you with others," the women are saying here in this scripture, "just let me be called by your last name." Sadly, even today some women are willing to sacrifice a whole lot just to have a man in their lives. But in spite of what statistics were reporting, they did not cause me to doubt God. My mind was set on the fact that if marriage was God's will for me, then not even my age or statistics would stop that from happening!

In the back of my mind also was the fear of the consequences of not waiting on God. Too many times, I got ahead of God. And too many times, I ended up bruised even more. I reasoned that although waiting was at times challenging, moving outside or moving ahead of God's timing made things more challenging and always made matters worse.

Of course there were days I got tired of waiting. Then there were days where the waiting didn't bother me. There were times I felt that God was being totally unfair. Then there were times when I relaxed in Him, knowing that everything, including my wedding date, was in His hand.

At those times where the wait seemed to smother the very life out of me, I had to hold on to God's unchanging hand for dear life! Sometimes, I was angry with God. Sometimes, I would shut myself off from others – just didn't want to be bothered. At other times, my heart ached, wondering why God was taking so long. I had to push and pray my own self through it! Many times the relief didn't come all of a sudden. BUT, it did come! God led me beside the still waters and refreshed my soul (Psalm 23:2-3). He lifted me out of that horrible pit (Psalm 40:1-2) of anxiety and gave me the strength to continue on in the wait. I didn't get it right every time, but the time came where I truly "got it right" and found sweet rest in His arms. Then the waiting was more bearable.

Now, I can truly say that it was worth the wait! The joy I experience now being married to the one that God had for me (that's the key) outweighs the hurt, pain, and frustrations that I experienced being single. I can truly testify that waiting time is not wasted time. God was preparing me to be the person He would have me to be. He gave me double for every heartache, frustration, and disappointment that I experienced as a single.

Waiting may try your patience to the limits. I mean to the limits! But, the benefits are huge! So I say to you wait on the Lord and be of good courage (Psalm 27:14) - and when you don't feel of "good courage" ask the Savior to help you, comfort, strengthen and keep you. He is willing to aide you and He will carry you through.

Also, know that during the waiting period two things ARE NOT options:
1. Settling for Mr. Wrong or Ms. Wrong. I'm sure you can tell me at least seven reasons why
2. Allowing bitterness to set up in you. The Bible says in Hebrews 12:15 that

bitterness defiles you. In other words, it dirties you up. It corrupts your soul. It defiles your sacrifices unto the Lord.

Consider the story of Ruth in the Bible when you feel bitterness trying to overtake you. She was widowed at a young age. On top of that no good prospects were in sight. On top of that she had no children by her husband. In biblical days, having children was a big thing. So here she was husbandless and childless. She had every right to be bitter, yet she continued to trust God and did not become weary in well-doing. Well, one day because of her unfailing trust and commitment to God, she was blessed to marry the most eligible bachelor in town. You talk about a fairytale ending! The man was attractive and rich! See, she got all of these things without aiming for any of them! She could have been bitter and allowed it to keep her from holding on to God. But, she didn't! She made a choice. She made the right choice. She made the choice to not become bitter, but to wait and trust God. In the end, she truly got double for her trouble! Since God is no respect of person (Acts 10:34), He will do the same for you. It is truly a blessing to wait on God!

Reflection

1. What are some of the benefits of waiting on God?

2. What are some of the consequences of not waiting on God?

3. Is it more important to have what you want or what God wants?

4. List five scriptures that can help strengthen you while in the wait.

Chapter 5

Wrong Roles

Our God in His infinite wisdom knew exactly what He was doing when He created man and woman as a method of keeping the world populated. He created both in His own image (Genesis 1:27). Each had distinct roles to carry out in the world, keeping things operating in an orderly fashion. Man was created to be the provider, the pursuer, the head of household (Ephesians 5:23). On the other hand, woman was created to be a nurturer, the pursued, man's help meet (Genesis 2:18).

It is when men and women step outside of the roles that God has given them that confusion, chaos and discontentment occur. Let's take a close look at Proverbs 18:22. It states that *Whoso findeth a wife, findeth a good thing, and obtaineth favour of the Lord.* This scripture clearly informs us that it is the man's role to do "the finding," not the woman's. Here lies a major area of frustration for single Christians. I mean a MAJOR one!

Today's society has reversed the roles. The movies show us that absolutely nothing is wrong with a woman trying to "hook up" with a man; trying to develop ways to garner a man's attention; trying to place themselves in a position where a man can notice them; come after them, even if it means buying them expensive gifts or pretending to buy them a gift under the guise of "friendship!" (Whew, another chapter by itself)! After all, this is not the 60's and it has become status quo for the woman to be the pursuer. What this spells out for the Christian single female is big time F-R-U-S-T-R-A-T-I-O-N in every sense of the word! Why? It goes against God's order. Take a look again at Proverbs 18:22. It clearly states *whoso findeth a* wife, not *whoso findeth a* husband. You feel me? In taking this route, my dear sister, more than likely you will come up empty-handed or get something you wish you could throw back. Initially, a man will appear flattered because of the attention you are giving him. But in the end, he'll become bored and label you as being "just like the others," "desperate," or "too aggressive."

When a woman can grasp this very important truth, they will surely find peace and realize they have the best role in the world – to sit back, look pretty, and allow the man to find and "woo" them. Let him buy the expensive gifts. Allow him to find out about your favorite spots and then position himself in them. Allow him to inquire about you to others. Just relax. Relax. Re-lax.

Now don't get me wrong, you don't have to play hard to get either. That will turn off a man as well. There are some simple, yet not over the top things you can do to let him know that you are interested. For instance, when he speaks to you, politely smile rather than ignore him thinking that by ignoring him you will really get him going. It might for a moment, but after awhile he'll tire out and turn his attention elsewhere.

Let's look again at Ruth's story. After Ruth and her mother-in-law, returned to Bethlehem, Ruth went to work in Boaz's (Naomi's wealthy kinsman) field in order to provide for her and Naomi. Ruth was such a woman of productivity. As she worked, she caught the eye of guess who? You got it Boaz. She caught Boaz's attention not as she found out about his hangout and went there strictly to catch his attention; not as she bought him expensive gifts, not as she asked him out on a date, but as she simply operated in her role as a caring daughter-in-law. I imagine that if she would have thrust herself on Boaz then he might have considered her to be "like all other women," simply after him for his wealth. This would not have been a very happy ending to this story for Ruth.

My dear woman of God, I cannot emphasize this enough. You have the easiest role in the world and that is simply to be found. If you trust God as you say you do, then you can trust Him to guide who He has for you to you. God doesn't need your help. Remember He knows all things and can do absolutely anything. Know that when a man is really interested in you, he will do all the chasing, asking for your number, asking for dates, everything – you won't have to do anything (more on this in a later chapter)! On the flip side, when a man is not that into you, you will know that as well. Stop ignoring the signs, running full speed, heart first!

When I met my husband, we already knew each other from working in the church. He was a stickler for punctuality and organization. One day I presented him with new music for the area for which he was over and because I was 2 days late, he refused to assist! He didn't even consider all the other times throughout the years that I had not been late. Boy was I upset! I vowed never to ask for his assistance again! Little did I know that one day he had developed an interest in me, and the rest is history!

I remembered the day when "he" made his interest known. I didn't have to do anything. He made the first step in everything – in asking for my number, in contacting me, in telling me about him, and much later on in asking me for a date. What did I do as all of this was taking place? I did NOT run behind him. I did NOT wait around in places at church where I knew he would pass by. I did not. I did not. Now, I knew not to be rude and a prude. After all, I was baiting a fish, lol! I was truly comfortable in the easy role, and you will be too. Ask God to calm you down. Ask Him to help you to operate in the role He has given you. Ask Him to help you not to step out of place. Ask Him to forgive you if you have and to help you move forward into the destiny He has created for you! If you're a male, you can join in this prayer as well. If you have been guilty of allowing women to chase you, ask God to forgive you and to help you step up to the role He has assigned you. In operating in your role, male or female, you will find your life more at ease, more peaceful, and a whole less stressful!

Reflection

1. Why do you think it is so important that we as men and women operate in the distinct role that God has given us when it comes to relationships?

2. Do you find it difficult at times to function in the role God has given you? If so, what are some things that you can do to help you in this area?

3. True or False. God created each of us with specific roles. It is when we step outside of this role, that confusion and frustration comes.

4. In your own words, what is meant by "chance rendezvous" vs. "divine timing?"

Chapter 6

The Unguarded Heart

The unguarded heart is another major source of discontentment and frustrations for single Christians, particularly with women. Because women are social creatures, caring, emphatic, nurturing and so forth, it's so easy for us to approach any relationship with our heart out first! But, ouch how this hurt when it's placed in the hands of the wrong person!

Let's say when a woman meets a guy who seems to have himself together. The guy says the right things, does the right things, and seems like a real gentleman. Within three weeks of the relationship, she begins to think to herself that "this could be the one." You begin to visualize your wedding gown, wedding colors, what would be a good month to get married in, and so forth. Never mind, you have only dated for three weeks and the relationship is far from turning into an engagement. Debby Jones and Jackie Kendall in their book *Lady in* Waiting call this "prenuptial fantasies." Then boom! There it goes! Heart in first! You don't give yourself enough time to fully check him out. Even if you notice things about him that are not kosher and that you don't particularly care about, you overlook them or begin to make excuses for him. You're too busy being excited about this new prospect, while your heart has plunged in deep!

The Bible in Proverbs 4:23 cautions us, man or woman, to *"Keep thy heart with all diligence; for out of it are the issues of life."* In other words, you have the responsibility for guarding your heart, keeping it out of harm's way. If I had really taken this scripture to heart in my early 20's, it would have saved me from a many heartaches. It hits the nail on the head when it comes to protecting oneself from relationship blues. The writer is clearly aware of the danger of giving out one's heart too fast. He's aware of the danger of placing your heart into the hands of the wrong individual. He is aware of the dangers of a broken heart. The aches of a broken heart can be so powerful that they have driven some to commit murder, others to kidnapping and others to commit suicide. This we've witness from stories in the news.

If you are in a situation where your heart has been given to the wrong individual, please seek God for deliverance, for an escape route. First Corinthians 10:13 says,

> There hath no temptation taken you but such as is common to man: but God is faithful, who will not suffer you to be tempted above ye are able; but will with the temptation make a way of escape that ye may be able to bear it.

This is a scripture of hope and victory because it lets you know that God can and will make a way of escape for you. With God, it doesn't matter how long or how deep you are in, He is able to deliver you.

Reflection

1. How can you protect your heart from relationship woes?

2. If you are in a hurtful relationship right now, do you believe that God can provide a way of escape for you as well as mend your broken heart?

3. What are some things you can do to help you control your heart and thoughts when first meeting someone?

4. According to Proverbs 4:23, whose responsibility is it to guard the heart?

   Ask God to show you ways in times past that you have been guilty of not protecting your heart. Then ask Him to teach you how to protect your heart in all things.

Chapter 7

He's/She's Not That Into You

Let's start with the man, since he is the head. What are a few signs that a man isn't really interested? Well, when you have to do all the calling, all the asking out, all the giving, these are clear signals; when you're always trying to 'figure out" where the relationship is headed – Are you friends or are you more? Does he really like you? What did he mean when he said this? What did he mean when he said that? When you are always in a position of trying to figure out what his intentions are, then he's really not that interested in you. Sure he likes you as a friend, but probably not more. Again, when he's that into you, he will show it and you will know it!

Likewise, when a woman says she will call you back but doesn't, particularly after a couple of weeks pass, then she's probably not that into you. When you have to repeatedly ask her when is she going out with you, and she either gives you a blank answer or changes the subject, then she's really not that interested in you. When you buy her gift after gift and all she says is a polite "Thank you" without ever reciprocating even when it's your birthday, then she's not that into you. This same scenario applies when a woman relentlessly buys a man several gifts without ever receiving anything in return.

Many times singles "settle" for relationships with individuals who are not interested in being more than friends because they don't want to be alone. They feel any man or woman is better than not having one. The signs are there but they keep pressing on hoping that things will change, hoping that he or she will begin to see them in another light, hoping for the better. However, I caution you here that when the signs are there, don't ignore them!

Here are some additional ones. You can say "I love you." They may simply respond with a "polite" smile. You can try to turn the conversation into talking about your relationship and its future, but they consistently act like they are not getting your hints or even change the conversation. They will tell you, "I'll call you later." But later never comes. When you ask about it (never mind they should have said something first since they were the ones who did not keep their word), they respond "I got busy doing something for my mother or my friend." When a person is really into you and they get tied up, they will send you some type of communication that day to inform you of what has happened. If it's the next day, you won't have to call and ask what happen. They will be the first to call, apologize and explain what happen.

Also, check out their mannerism when you all go out. Are they focused on you or are they busy checking out every nice looking individual that walks by even while talking to you? Don't misunderstand me here. We all notice other attractive individuals even when we're out with that special someone in our lives. But when that other individual gets more attention then you, when you have to repeat several times what you have said because your date's attention is focused on the other person, then you need to take note of that.

Another indication that a person isn't really interested in you is when they don't like to commit to plans and if they do it's at the very last minute. I remember dating a guy once who had no problem making plans with his friends, but when it came to us he didn't want to commit to plans. This guy and I were not even "boyfriend/girlfriend." We were in the initial stages of talking and finding out about one another. Well, needless to say after about three of those incidences, I knew he wasn't worth the time of my day. I had no problem ignoring future calls from him! However, sometimes singles continue in this cycle with hopes that the person will change. Some go so far as to make excuses for them. But in order to save yourself from more embarrassment, disgust and frustration see it for what it is.

What about the individual who puts off introducing you to his or her family or friends over and over again? When it's time for the family gatherings or gatherings with friends, rather than including you, they don't. And when you ask about it, they dance around the subject. When someone really likes you they want to show you off to the world as oppose to always wanting to meet you at places or go to places where there is no chance they will run into others who they know.

Moreover, when an individual is not supportive of you – your ideas, your career, your goals in life, this can be another indication that they are not that interested. When a person is truly interested, they are interested in your thoughts and what you have to say. They are interested in what makes you tick, your ideas, your hopes, your dreams - even if none of these interest them.

What does it mean when a person is not that into you? Does it mean you are a bad person? Does it mean that you are unattractive? Does it mean that something is wrong with you? No, it does not mean any of these things. It simply means that you're not the one for them and they are not the one for you. When a person really likes you, even if you're not listed among the most beautiful people in the world, it doesn't matter to them. They still would like to know more about you. The Bible even speaks about being unequally yolk with individuals (2 Corinthians 6:14). Although the specific reference is to unbelievers, I think we can also apply this principle in general to unbalanced relationships.

So what should you do? You have two choices here. You can make excuses, thereby incurring more pain; more disappointment; more hurt. Or you can walk away. Of course option number two is most difficult especially, if you have invested a lot into the "relationship." Difficult it may be, but not IMPOSSIBLE. Again, with God, there are no things impossible. There is always a way of escape! Remember that. Also, ask yourself if it is fair for you to settle for less the rest of your life. Or if it's better that you wake up, smell the coffee, and reach (with the help of God) for the better that you deserve. A person who likes you just as much or even more than you like them will have no problem making sacrifices in the relationship. Just as it comes easy for you to make sacrifices, it will come easy for them.

Reflection

1. Have you ever been in a relationship with another person who was "not that into you?"

   How did it make you feel?

2. Are you still in that relationship?   If yes, ask yourself, "Is this how I want to be treated for the rest of my life?"

You may argue, "Dr. Dee I have tried to get out. I want to get out." My response to you is that when you really want something bad enough, you will do what it takes to get it. If you lack the strength, ask God to strengthen you. It's yours for the asking Matthew 7:7 – *Ask and it shall be given; seek and ye shall find; knock and the door shall be open.*

Look at the movie *Madea's Family Reunion* by Tyler Perry. No matter how her sister tried to tell the young lady that her abusive fiancé was no good for her, she remained in the relationship. But tell me, what did she do when she really got sick and tired of being sick and tired?

Chapter 8

Well-Meaning Friends

Well-meaning friends can be another source of single life frustrations. Although, well-meaning in their intentions, their comments and actions can create a world of frustration for you. What do I mean? I'm going to focus on single women here because it seems not only is it easier for us to let our hearts get ahead of us, but our thoughts as well.

Let's say you see a guy that you are interested in. Well a well-meaning friend may say something to you like, "Go ahead. Get his number. He likes you." Although trying to help, their suggestion goes against all the rules! If he's interested, he will ask for your number, not the other way around. Remember the chapter on *Wrong* Roles? Well, this suggestion goes against your God-given role.

Or a well-meaning friend, rather than caution you to be careful and take it slowly as she hears you rant and rave about this new guy that you have been dating for two weeks, may join in boosting your hopes even more by saying things like "Girl, he may be the one. I can see you getting married. I can even visualize myself in the bridesmaid dresses." "What colors do you want for your wedding?" Talk such as this will most certainly cause the single woman's mind to dive into a world of daydreams and wishful thinking, running the risk of setting her up for more disappointments. My goodness, the dating relationship is only two weeks old!

Ok, let's flip the script here and focus on young men. Suppose you meet a young lady who seems to be everything that you have wanted – she looks good, she's shaped good, she's smart and seems to have her head on straight. You tell your friends about her after two dates. Rather than your friends cautioning you to pray about it, they add to the "high" you're on by saying, "Man, she could be the one. She seems to have everything going for her. She's so fine. You should keep this one." Although well-meaning in their intent, the relationship is far too young to determine who should keep who. Two dates will not provide you with everything you need to know about a person. Even if an individual seems to have everything going for them, you still need to guard your heart and proceed with caution regardless to the advice of well-meaning friends. Although your friends desire to see you happy, they can play an important role in helping you maintain your head, your heart and your emotions while dating.

As you prayerfully ask God about a potential mate, guard yourself against the advice of well-meaning friends who want you to have the best, but whose suggestions may push you into a world of hurt in the long run. Ladies, if your friends suggest that you get his number since they can tell that he really likes you, you can help calm things down by politely replying, "No. That's his job. I can wait." Likewise men, if your friends suggest to you that it's a good chance that she's the one only after two dates, you can help calm things down by politely replying, "Yeah. We've been on two great dates. But, I'm keeping my head on straight here. It's too early to tell."

REFLECTION

Meditate on Proverbs 3:7; Ephesians 5:15-17; and Ecclesiastes 3:1. What are these scriptures saying to you?

Chapter 9

The Heat Is On

Acting improperly when your passionate urges overwhelm you is a huge source of single life frustration. Why? It violates God's word (1 Corinthians 6:18-20). It doesn't cement the relationship, as some wrongly think. Instead, you'll end up losing much ground in the relationship as you struggle with feelings of 1) guilt – because you have let God and yourself down, 2) worry – wondering if you're pregnant or have contacted some type of disease or if the guy will move on since he has gotten what he wanted; 3) fear – that others will find out; that your partner won't feel the same about you anymore; and 4) regret – because rather than causing him to stay, it caused him to leave. You're left feeling abandoned and used - feelings that you won't get over so quickly. And, also regret because you have violated your commitment to God.

Indeed, engaging in sexual activity in a relationship does NOT guarantee you happiness and everlasting love. When it comes to your body as a single man or woman, it belongs to God. God has given clear guidelines in His word – to protect it, to cherish it, to keep it set apart for His service, to keep you from living with shame, guilt and disappointment (1 Corinthians 7:32-35; 2 Timothy 2:22). No matter how much you feel "obligated" to show your love physically to the person who you are dating; regardless to how Hollywood or the world says it's the normal thing to do, it's a violation of God's word. Any violation of God's word, spells trouble. Romans 6:23 says, *For the wages of sin is death....* Also, Proverbs 14:12 says, *There is a way which seemeth right unto man, but the end thereof is death.* Either way, the end is "death" for you. The pleasure of sin may seem exciting and fulfilling initially, but in the end it will lead to unfulfillment and separation from God.

I can't tell you of the many stories that I have heard from individuals who were exasperated, at wits end as they struggled with the guilt of having sex outside of marriage. Some felt like it was the only way they could keep their partner. Some admitted that it was a mistake, that rather than add to the relationship it took away from it. Others felt used, as the other person moved on to someone else. Still others, desired to turn to talk to someone in the church, but wouldn't for fear that they would be looked down upon, no longer deemed "usable" for the Master's use.

Although engaging in sex outside of marriage is a source of single life frustrations, keep in mind if you have fallen in this area there is restoration for you. Perhaps you're living with guilt because you have already been sexually involved with the person you are dating or persons you have dated. Well our God, is a God of forgiveness. If you repent and ask for His forgiveness, as the scripture hath said *he is faithful and just to forgive us and cleanse us from all unrighteousness* (1 John 1:9). God even takes it a step further and says *he will remember our sins no more* (Jeremiah 31:34). However, remember also that we do not continue in sin that His grace may abound (Romans 6:1). Rather, we accept the forgiveness that He offers with the intent and determination to not fall again, choosing to enjoy the close fellowship we have with Him rather than the pleasure of sin for a season (Hebrews 11:25).

Maybe you even feel like the Apostle Paul, as if you're in an ongoing cycle of falling and getting back up, falling and getting back up. This destructive habit seems to be getting the best of you. The Apostle Paul said in Romans 7:15-19 that the good that he would do, he did not. That the evil that he didn't want to do; he did. Paul said that when he would do good, evil was present with him. Yet, with God in the equation, He ends in chapter eight on a victorious note. He says in Romans 8:24-25 (a), *O wretched man that I am! Who shall deliver me from the body of this death? I thank God through Jesus Christ our Lord.* He says through Jesus Christ that whatever he was going through which caused him to choose wrong over right time and time again, he could gain the victory by leaning on, depending on and trusting Jesus to carry Him through! Like the Apostle Paul, you can too! Truly with God in the equation in any of our lives, we are never left without hope regardless to how many times we haven't got it right (Jeremiah 32:27). Know that if you're in this self-defeating cycle, you can still walk out with the victory!

The old saints often said "God will keep you if you want to be kept." When I first joined the holiness church, I didn't understand fully what that meant. The struggles I experienced were at times intense. However, in the process of time I came to understand completely what they were saying. They were saying that if a person had the mind, will and desire for God to keep them from falling, then He would do exactly that (Jude 24). That if the individual cooperated with God, by not placing themselves in positions where they were tempted beyond measure; by building a solid foundation through bible reading and prayer; by being involved in the church and hanging around friends who really meant Jesus, God would keep them.

Now for some this is not to say it's going to be as easy as 1, 2, 3 then presto, you won't have the struggle in your flesh anymore! It will be trying. But you can have victory. At times, you may simply want to give in to your desires, yet even in those times you can still have victory if you turn your attention from what you want to what God desires for you to do.

Let me add note of caution here. You seriously want to watch your thoughts to also help safeguard you in this area. As the Bible instructs you to guard your heart, you must also guard your thoughts. Loading your mind over and over with thoughts such as, "I need someone to hold me;" "I just want to be held by someone;" "I just need one good kiss" - will do nothing to help you stand when the heat is on. Instead, those thoughts must be cast down IMMEDIATELY! I emphasize immediately because the longer you allow yourself to dwell on them, the harder they will be to discard and the more difficult it will be for you to overcome. Philippians 4:8 tells us, *Finally, brethren, whatsoever things are true, whatsoever things are honest, whatsoever things are just, whatsoever things are pure, whatsoever things are lovely, whatsoever things are of good report; if there be any virtue, and if there be any praise, think on these things.* These are the type of thoughts you should allow your mind to dwell on.

If you simply have to say, "Jesus" over and over to help you get through, then do that. Sometimes, I would get up and get busy. I would go visit one of my friends or family members and stay until all I could do was go home and get straight in the bed, lol! Other times (and I laugh now), I would call my mom on the phone over and over. I'm sure she wondered why I kept calling back to back, not wanting anything. It's funny now.

But it was serious back then! I was trying to maintain! Have you ever heard the song "I'm running for my life? If anybody asks you, what's the matter with me............I'm running for my life! Well that was me!

Additionally, meditating on scriptures that deal with God's help, God's deliverance and God's grace will help sustain you during trying times such as these. Now, on the real? Sometimes the last thing you want to do is pray and meditate. You want what you want! But, it is the BEST thing for you to do and what you should do to keep you from cluttering your life up with more frustration and heartache. Although initially it may not seem like these scriptures are doing much to quiet your passion, continue to read and meditate upon them regardless. Remember the word is life and the word gives light! It will give you sustaining power. Also remember that everything that feels good isn't working for your good. Overeating ice cream, may feel good, but it isn't working for your good, especially if you face health challenges. The word of God is always right. It commands you to wait until you marry before engaging in sex for it's better to marry than to burn (1 Corinthians 7:9).

REFLECTION

1. How do you handle it when the "heat is on?"

2. Are there some scriptures which you can draw upon for strength during testing time? Please list them here.

3. If you have fallen in this area and feel that you can in no wise lift yourself up, read Luke 13:11-13; Isaiah 40:29. What are these scriptures saying to you?

4. What does James 1:13 mean to you?

Chapter 10

But He/She's a Good Person

Okay. Let me take a deep breath before I begin here. Let's revisit one of the scriptures that I mentioned earlier. Second Corinthians, chapter 6, verse 14 says,

> *Be ye not unequally yoked together with unbelievers: for what fellowship hath righteousness with unrighteousness? and what communion hath light with darkness?*

What does this mean for you? It means that regardless to how you may argue that the person you met is a good person - good morals, good values and good to you, if he or she is not saved, then you are setting yourself up for potential heartbreak. The Bible is clear here when it warns us to be not unequally yolk with unbelievers. Why? Although they may be a morally good person, their values can eventually clash with yours. To you going to church, attending conferences and prayer shut-ins is great because it helps strengthen your walk with the Lord. To them it may appear "over the top." To you, the Bible provides clear direction on sex outside of marriage, avoiding tempting situations and so forth. However, to them there is nothing wrong with sex outside of marriage because it shows how much you love one another. Initially, they may tell you that they understand and won't get in the way of your service to the Lord, but in the end it may prove too much for them.

Moreover, using the argument that "at least they go to church" is not good enough either. In order to protect your heart, the bottom line is are they a man or woman after God's own heart; one who not only goes to church, but who strives to live for God all they know how. I can't tell you of the many sad stories I have heard about women and men dating an individual who they say "go to church," only to find out that this individual was the "enemy" in disguise.

I know of two good Christian friends of mine, one male and one female. With the guy, he felt he had found the woman of his dreams. She was attractive and really liked him. They did everything together. They went to church, enjoyed church activities and attending other outings. She was nice and became a Christian after meeting him. No, she didn't become Christian to get him. In this case, I think she really liked him and wanted to share in His love for Christ. Eventually, they got married. About two years later, they divorced. Why? She felt that his commitment to God was much more than what she was ready for.

In the case of my Christian female friend, she met a guy who was not saved. She said that he was nice looking, fun to be around and was very good to her. I remember her telling me rather justifying the fact that she dated him because he treated her better than any Christian man she had ever dated. I cautioned her to proceed slowly because although he treated her well, it concerned me that he was not saved. They dated for about two years. She fell in love with him and they talked about marriage. Eventually, he broke it off with her. Her commitment to God and ministry was more than what he was ready for. My friend was devastated.

Perhaps you know of stories where everything worked out– where one person was saved and the other unsaved, and the result was a happy ending for them by the grace of God. I feel that those instances are VERY rare. I hear of more stories where the ending was the opposite. Remember, nothing is written in the word of God to harm us. Rather, what's written in God's word is to keep us from harm; to keep us from heartbreak; to prevent us from taking paths that will lead to devastation in the end. You should remind yourself of these very things when tempted to be angry at God because you feel He is keeping you from enjoying life. If God tells us not to be unequally yolk in our relationships in life, He is doing so for our own good. Initially, the relationship may start out great. You may seem to be having the time of your life. But in the end, as your morals and values begin to clash because yours is Word-base and his or hers is worldly-base, you will end up with a crushed heart.

Even if you experience a period of weeks or months of not going out on a date, resist the urge to compromise your standards for the sake of "just one date." Your standard must be higher than "at least they go to church." A date with the wrong person can cause you to wish you had no date at all. Besides, you can slow your roll here. Didn't God promise that no good thing will He withhold from them who walk upright (Psalm 84:11)? So.....if He promised it, shall He not make good on it (Numbers 23:19)? Ask God to help you take it down a couple of notches and find rest in Him.

Also, do not give in to the temptation of accepting dates with unbelievers thinking that they will change or that you can change them. You're wrong! Many times the opposite occurs. Rather than you influencing them, they will influence you. Once again the Bible is clear, *Be not deceived* (in other words, "Don't get it twisted"): *evil communications corrupt good manners.* (1 Corinthians 15:33). Guarding your heart, requires you to be sensitive to the leading of the Lord, and for you to base your standards not on what looks good or feels good, but on God's word.

REFLECTION

1. Have you ever dated an individual who was an unbeliever because they treated you well?   What were the end results?

2. What does 2 Corinthians 6:14 mean to you?

How can you guard yourself against this?

3. Do you believe that the commandments of God are to hurt you or help you? Explain.

4. If you believe they are to help you, what are some ways you can begin putting them into action, particularly when it comes to living as a single Christian?

Chapter 11

The Single Professional

A final source of frustration that I will discuss comes from the single professional. By this I mean, individuals who are single, hold professional jobs or good paying jobs, who are educated, well dressed, live in nice places and who drive nice cars. This group of individuals deal with frustrations that stem from two sources: 1) fear of the odds being against them relative to marriage since many are viewed as "unapproachable" and not in need of anything or anybody and, 2) trust issues - always wondering in the back of their mind if the potential prospect is dating them for what they have as oppose to who they are.

To you I say two words: **Trust God**. Ladies, the one God has for you will not be afraid to approach you regardless to your status or success in life. The one He has in store for you will like you for you, not your success. You won't be intimidating to him, but admired by him. Your strength will not be a turn off to him, but something he respects. Men, your success will not be a turn off or turn on for her. True enough she will be impressed by what God has blessed you with; however you will not have to worry about her being a "gold digger."

Whether you are a single male or female, Proverbs 3:5-6 comes to into play here. It says to *Trust in the Lord with <u>all</u> thine heart; lean not unto thine own understanding. In all thy ways acknowledge him and he shall direct thy* path. Ask God about everything. Even before you accept a date, ask God. He has promised to lead and guide you into all truth (John 16:13) even concerning your mate. With Him on your side, you don't have to worry about being taking advantage of UNLESS you ignore the leading of His Holy Spirit. Psalm 37:23 says *The steps of a good man are ordered by the Lord...* Truly, God will lead you in the path of righteousness (Psalm 23:1) if you allow Him to; if you don't allow your heart, emotions and feelings to run ahead of you. Be anxious for nothing, God tells you, but in <u>everything</u> by prayer and supplication with thanksgiving, let your request be made known unto Him (Philippians 4:16). You won't have to bombard your mind with questions like "Are they after me or what I have?" "I wonder if I can trust them?" "Do they really have my best interest at heart?" See with God at center, there is no guessing game involved. There is no confusion, but peace (1 Corinthians 14:33). He makes things clear and very clear.

Ladies, perhaps you have even read statistics that report that it is more challenging for the professional female to get a suitable mate more so than others. Well, my questions to you are: 1) "Whose report will you believe? The statistics or God?" and 2) "What can God not do?" He can and will do anything, but fail. If He can cause a big red sea to part (Exodus 14); the mouth of hungry lions to shut and not devour Daniel (Daniel 6); keep the fire from burning the Hebrew boys who were thrown into the fire with no way out (Daniel 3); feed 5,000 men not including women and children with only two fish and five loaves of bread (Matthew 14), then He certainly can bring a man into your life, that is not after what you have, but after His own heart. The same goes for the single professional male who puts his complete trust in God.

REFLECTION

Ask yourself:
- Is your trust in God or in who you are or what you have?
- Is your trust in God or in the statistics that you read about on the availability of good men or women?
- Is your trust in God or the callous words uttered by your associates who tell you that you might as well give up? That there are no good men or women out there.

If your trust is in anything but God, then you are trusting in the wrong thing. Write down 5 steps you can implement now that will help you learn to trust God more.

Chapter 12

Self Reliance – vs – Savior Reliance

To help you better cope with many of the frustrations that you feel as a single ask yourself this important question: "Am I self-reliant or Savior-reliant?" In other words, are you more dependent on yourself – what you think, how you feel, your own strength, your own reasoning power more so than you are on Christ's strength, His word, His guidance, His instructions to you? If you are more self-reliant as oppose to Savior-reliant, then you are living in defeat already.

The Bible says that *in (me)* that is the flesh, *dwelleth no good thing* (Romans 7:18). So if no good thing dwells in the flesh, how can you and I depend upon ourselves to make wholesome decisions? How can we rely on ourselves to make moral choices for us in testing situations; to give us the strength to say 'no' when everything in us is saying yes?; to lead and guide us anywhere, exception to destruction? If you want to get a handle on some of the frustrations you are experiencing then focus on becoming more Savior-reliant as oppose to self-reliant –

leaning and depending totally on Christ for everything – for strength to overcome, for strength to wait, to help you determine who is and who is not dating material, and so on and so forth. As the scripture hath said *Commit thy way unto the Lord; trust also in him, and he shall bring it to pass* (Psalm 37:5).

Focus on getting to know Christ in a more intimate way. I promise you, if you try this, you will love it! He will take such good care of you. He'll be that friend who sticks closer than a brother (Proverbs 18:24). He'll give you favor with those in high places. He'll provide for all your needs, as well as your desires. Psalm 37:4 admonishes you to *Delight thineself also in the Lord: and he shall give you the desires of your heart* (Psalm 37:4). Delight means to take pleasure in; find satisfaction or fulfilment in getting to know someone. When you delight in the Lord, your desires become aligned with His will. When your desires become aligned with His will, then you ask for things that are according to His will. When you ask for the things that are according to His will, you can be confident that He hears and will grant what you ask (1 John 5:14).

Many times we come up shorthanded in life because we short hand God. *Preach Dr. Dee!* God should have His rightful place in your life and that is first and foremost! You may argue, "Well, He does Dr. Dee! I know Him well because I do so much in the name of the Lord. I'm always at church. I pray. I always volunteer for something at church and I am very committed to the auxiliary that I am a part of." But to you I ask, "Do you really *know* Him?" Paul said that *I may know Him, and the power of his resurrection, and the fellowship of his sufferings, being made conformable unto His death* (Philippians 3:10). Hosea 6:3 says, *Then shall we know, if we follow on to know the Lord?* (Who are you following? Yourself or the Lord?). We can do all the right things, but that doesn't mean that God has His rightful place in our lives. It doesn't mean that we really know Him. When He is in the right place, when our relationship with Him is first and foremost, then many of the heartaches, and disappointments that we experience in life are avoided.

So, I challenge you to become more Savior-reliant as oppose to self-reliant. I encourage you to spend quality time developing a relationship with God as you would with someone you are dating. Remember how you can't stand to be a part from them? How they are on your mind constantly throughout the day? How you think of ways that you can make life better for them? How you try your best not to offend them? Well, treat God in this same way. Have constant thoughts about Him throughout the day – living for Him as best you know, pleasing Him in how you interact with co-workers, family members, friends, etc.; thinking of ways you can improve in your relationship with Him; ways you can better serve Him. A quality relationship with Him will pay huge dividends in your life and in your relationships. Instead of being upset with Him for holding back on the thing you want most, use this time to really get to know Him. When you get to really know Him, You will have no problem relying on Him because you will know that He really does have your best interest at heart.

For a moment in my life, I really wrestled with following God with all my heart verses following my own desires. When someone admonished me to get to know Him better, I would think to myself, "Well, I know that. Tell me something else." But when I actually made up my mind to lay my wants and desires to side, focusing truly on living for God, I can't explain to you how much peace, comfort, fun and rest I found in Him! I had heard others say that when you have a close relationship with God, the things that really use to bother you suddenly begin to lose their significance. But then I experienced it one day for myself! And boy, oh boy was it a blessing to finally have such comfort in Him!

So again I admonish you to allow your Creator and heavenly Father to truly be Lord of your life. Contrary to what you may think and how you may feel at times, He desires to do you good, to give you an expected end (Jeremiah 29:11).

But, as it is written, Eye hath not seen, nor ear heard, neither have entered into the heart of man hath prepared for them that love him, the things which God hath prepared for them that love him. (1 Corinthians 2:9).

Reflection

1. In what ways have you been self-reliant?

2. In what ways have you been Savior-reliant?

Purpose to move the items you've listed under self-reliant to your Savior-reliant list.

3. List seven scriptures that admonish you to rely on God for His help.

Chapter 13

Know Your Worth

Knowing your worth will further help you deal with single life frustrations. You must not only know it, but believe in it! If you don't think that you are worth anything, you will settle for anything. You won't think that you deserve any good thing neither will you expect great things to come your way! You must know your worth!

Janet Zimmerman in her article, *The Journey to True Worth Starts Within,* writes:

> The value you place on yourself and what you think about yourself determines whether or not you know your full worth. Answering these questions shows what and how you think, and feel and value about yourself. Do you...
>
> 1. Settle for less than you deserve?
> 2. Chase love that isn't yours?
> 3. Make someone your priority while you're their option?

4. Care more about what others think of you than you think about yourself?
5. Spend time with people who can't commit or are already in a relationship?
6. Think that "I'm not enough."
7. Put your life on hold because you're waiting to see what the other person will do?
8. Go along with your partner whims instead of expressing what you'd like?
9. Seek love, appreciation and approval from your partner instead of finding them within?
10. Rationalize your partner's bad behavior even though it hurts you?
11. Manipulate or control your partner?
12. Let your partner's words and actions determine your mood?

She goes on to say that if "yes" or "sometimes" are your answers to any of these questions, other people and external circumstances are determining your worth. The good news is that knowing where you stand is empowering. You can begin to improve your own worth. Well stated, Ms. Zimmerman! There is such liberation in the words she has written. As we would say, "she's telling it like it is."

As I mentioned earlier, the Bible is our roadmap, our compass in life. It also has much to say about your worth. Did you know that? The word of God says that you are created in the very image of God (Genesis 1:27). That alone is enough to let you know that you're no junk! That you are prime cut! It says you are royal - not a wreck, chosen - not a mistake, holy and peculiar, not like everybody else (1 Peter 2:9). In other words, you are all that and much more! That's the Word! You are so high on the totem pole with God, that He gave the only Son that He had so that you could enjoy a right relationship with Him (John 3:16). That's how important you are! God says you are indeed the *apple of his eye* (Psalm 17:8).

Again, when you know your worth, then you won't settle for mess. When you know your worth and a guy or woman is not that into you, you will be the first to "keep it moving," knowing that it will be dangerous for you to park there! When you know your worth, you won't settle for a man or woman who treats you poorly just for the sake of having someone. No indeed! You won't settle for second best but will gladly wait on God's best! When you know your worth, others will know it too and treat you accordingly.

REFLECTION

If you struggle in the area of self-worth, here are some practical principles to apply to help you in this area.

1. Read what the Word of God says daily about your self-worth. I mentioned several scriptures in this chapter. Meditate on these verses daily and each time you meditate ask God to help you receive what His word says about you.

2. Never underestimate the power of your thoughts. They determine how you feel, which then will determine your behaviors and actions. Begin to think positive thoughts about yourself! Come on you can do it! Start off making a list of 10 things that you admire about you. It could be your strengths or something you have accomplished, no matter how big or small it is. Each day purpose to add two additional things

that come to mind. Use this list as a daily source of meditation, repeating them out loud. Allow them to sink in your spirit until you can feel the change in how you view yourself.

3. Begin casting down negative thoughts you have about yourself. For example, before the thought "I am weak," can play out in your mind, cast it down. Replace this thought with something positive about you or something positive that you are doing. Do this each day for the next three weeks. Write down how this makes you feel and how it affects your self-esteem.

Chapter 14

Know That You Are Loved

Along with knowing your self-worth, knowing that you are loved will also help you better cope with some of the challenges you are dealing with. Many times an individual looks for love in all the wrong places because they are looking for love from someone, anyone, they believe can give it to them. But my dear woman or man of God, you must know that there is someone who loves you dearly. His name is Jesus. Ephesians 3:17-18 says,

> *That Christ may dwell in your hearts by faith; that ye, being rooted and grounded in love. May be able to comprehend with all saints, what is the breadth, and length, and depth and height: And to know the love of Christ, which passeth knowledge, that ye might be filled with all the fullness of God.*

That's deep! God has such a deep love for you. It's bigger than your imagination and deeper than any longing you may have. Romans 5:8 says, *But God commendeth his love toward us, in that, while we were yet sinners, Christ died for the ungodly.* Now that's love! That means when you and I were enemies with God, He still sent His only Son to die for our sins.

If you feel void of love in your life, ask God to help you receive the love He already has for you. The love He has for you is not to work against you, but it's working for you. His love is unlike man's love. There are no strings attached. His love doesn't expect you to shower Him with gifts or give of yourself in ungodly ways to prove your love for Him. Neither does He withdraw it at any time because you made Him angry or you did something He didn't like. It is unconditional.

REFLECTION

Meditate on the statement "God's love is unconditional." Write down what you believe it is saying. Write down how it makes you feel.

Chapter 15

Get a Life, Please

I'm sure you have heard this over and over again. Well here it is again for the third, fourth, maybe even the 10th time – get a life! Look at this way, are you drawn to an individual who seems boring, who doesn't have a life, who sucks life out of you because he or she has nothing going on for themselves? Well neither are they! You need a life - things to do, places to visit, people to see, goals to accomplish, busying yourself in the work of the Lord. A man can sense when you don't have anything going for yourself, but him. Likewise, a woman can too. And it's a turn off for both!

Consider the example of Ruth earlier. She was busy working in the field when Boaz noticed her. She wasn't at home feeling sorry for herself, wishing that some man would come and rescue her, take her out to dinner or a movie. But she was busy taking care of herself and her mother-in-law. Then there is the love story of Isaac and Rebekah in Genesis 24. Rebekah was busy carrying out her chores when she was noticed by Isaac's servant.

Getting involved will mean several important things for you: 1) less time staring at the wall wishing you had someone special 2) less time struggling with the dictates of your flesh 3) less time trying to change a man or woman who is not that interested in you, and 4) less time focusing on your single life frustrations. Wouldn't you call those important?

I can't tell you how fulfilling it was for me to busy myself doing things for the Lord, as well as pursue educational goals and other personal goals I had. I was proud of myself as a single woman for the things God allowed me to accomplish. It made me feel good when others remarked that I had it going on; that I had my head on straight; that I wasn't waiting to get married to start living, I was living right now! It made me feel good that I made God, my family and friends proud by using my time wisely when I was single.

Now that I'm married, at times I reflect on the freedom I had to pursue my goals and am so thankful God afforded me that time.

Now, I didn't over-do it, meaning I didn't fill my life with so many things to accomplish that I lost focus. But, I recognized the importance of being involved. It saved me from many frustrating moments. It gave me somewhere else to channel my energies and focus. See, when we get our focus off ourselves and what we do not have, it makes life more enjoyable.

Note also that getting involved also includes preparing yourself physically, mentally and spiritually for a mate. A great investment of your time! Just as you spend time and attention to adorning yourself with the latest fashions, with making sure everything is matching to a "T-" your lipstick, nail polish, toenail polish, your shoes, men - your ties and socks, and so forth, you should spend time also adorning yourself with the fruit of the Spirit (Galatians 5:22-23). Also, spend time improving yourself physically by getting into shape if need be. If you have been complaining that your waistline has stretched ten to fifteen inches past what you want it to be, don't you think it's about time you begin to work on it? Channel your energies also toward preparing yourself mentally, emotionally and spiritually – asking God to take away mental baggage and emotional scarring from previous relationships and to help you do things that will cause your soul to prosper in Him (3 John 1:2). All of these things will only work in your best interest AND in the best interest of your future relationship.

Ask yourself: "Is my life on hold until I have someone to hold? (Debby Jones & Jackie Kendall)

REFLECTION

1. Are you allowing "self-focus" to prevent you from moving on in life?

2. List some of the things – goals, dreams, aspirations that you have put on the back burner that you can now involve yourself in.

3. Try this exercise. Instead of giving in to your single-life frustrations focus more on "giving". That is, the moment you become overwhelmed with frustrations, purpose to do something for someone else. It can be sending an encouraging text; calling a friend who is having trouble at work; or taking an elderly person to the store. The point is take the focus off you and place it on someone else. Each time you implement this strategy write down what it does for you - how it makes you feel; how it helps you during frustrating times. Use this list as a source of encouragement during times of despair.

CHAPTER 16

Know You're in the Right Place

What do I mean? You've asked God time and time again "Lord, why am I still single?" You've even blamed yourself for things you have done or failed to do which you believe have prevented you from getting married. Perhaps you've felt as if you missed the one God sent your way too busy focusing on the one who has been stringing you along. Although you may feel that you are in the "wrong" place at this time in your life, know that you are right where God wants you to be. Remember that God is always in control! If He had wanted to bless you with your spouse by now, He very well could have. Have you ever thought of it that way? So if you are still single, then perhaps there is a reason(s) God has allowed it to be so. However, you still may want to "check" yourself to make sure it is nothing that you are doing that is causing you to remain in this state.

As trying as it may be, instead of blaming God; instead of blaming yourself; instead of despising your single state, ask

God to help you accept and embrace your singleness. Remember, God is able to do anything. Surely helping you to be content is not too hard for Him!

Know that being single is not a curse. It is not a deadly disease in which there is no cure. Again, we are instructed by the Word of God to be <u>anxious</u> for nothing, but to pray about everything (Philippians 4:6). Although there may be those, even in Christian circles, who may cause you to feel inferior because you are not married, that something is wrong with you because you're not married, take comfort in knowing that you are where God wants you to be, and He loves you right where you are. He doesn't think any less of you because you are single. He doesn't rank one state higher than the other. People may, but God celebrates both states.

Also, as I mentioned earlier, keep in mind that marriage does not mean eternal bliss. It doesn't mean it would put an end to some of the woes you're experiencing in your single life. It is not a cure for loneliness or love. There are some who are married but still feel lonely and unloved. Know that at the appointed time, if it is God's will that you marry, He will allow it to happen. He, not you, knows what's best for you.

REFLECTION

1. Have you ever asked, "Lord, why am I still single?" What was His response?

2. Have others ever made you feel poorly because you were not married? How did you handle this?

3. Write down some productive ways you can handle this from this point forward.

Chapter 17

Is Something Wrong With Me?

From my own experience and in talking to others, singles are oftentimes told "All you need is Jesus. You don't need anyone or anything else. Just concentrate on Him." While the meaning of this statement is to remind singles to direct their time and energy into developing a close relationship with the Lord, it has left some feeling flustered and frustrated because they feel they are "cheating" on their commitment to God; that they are "shortchanging" God because not all of their focus is on Jesus. Some of their focus is on their inner desire to have a mate. Some have even felt that others who made this statement were being hypocritical because while making the statement, they themselves had spouses.

Please know that NOTHING is wrong with you for desiring companionship. It's a natural desire that God has given you. You're not "shortchanging" your relationship with God just because you have these thoughts and feelings. Even the Lord said that it is good for man not to be alone

(Genesis 2:18). Perhaps it would be better stated if it is said that, "Although Jesus can satisfy our every need, there is nothing wrong with desiring to be married."

The problem comes in when your desire to be married is your ONLY focus, day in and day out; when you can't grow in your relationship with Christ because you are more concerned with having a man or woman in your life; when you can't move forward because you are consumed with trying to figure out when you're going to get married; who will it be; how long will you have to wait. Then it becomes an issue and a source of much frustration for you.

When these longings come, turn again to God. Ask Him to help calm them down, so that they don't overwhelm you to the point that you become depressed, discouraged or stressed. Even if you have to ask Him several times a day; several times within an hour, ask Him. He delights to meet you at your point of need. As the scripture says, *For we have not an high priest which cannot be touched with the feeling of our infirmities; but was in all points tempted as we, yet without sin* (Hebrews 4:15).

REFLECTION

1. How do you feel about the statement: All you need is Jesus?

2. Have you ever felt that you were "shortchanging" God because while you loved Him on one hand, you had thoughts and longings for Him to bless you with a mate on the other?

3. What is meant by the scripture *My God shall supply all my need according to His riches in glory by Christ Jesus* (Philippians 4:19)?

Chapter 18

Living Above Single Life Frustrations

Is there a point you may ask where you can live above single life frustrations? The answer lies with YOU. Not only do you hold the key, but you are the key in living your life to the fullest as a single, a principle that I teach in all of my coaching sessions.

Know that any goal worth achieving will require 5 key things: patience, commitment, perseverance, faith and prayer.

Patience – You won't get there overnight. Some habits have been long-established and will not be easily broken right away. *In your patience possess ye your souls* (Luke 21:19).
Commitment – You must recognize that there will be times of victory and times of loss. However if you remain committed to achieving your goals, even during times of setback, victory will be yours. *Therefore, my beloved brethren, be ye stedfast, unmoveable, always abounding in the work of the Lord, forasmuch as ye know that your*

labour is not in vain in the Lord (1 Corinthians 15:58).

Perseverance – Realize that this journey is worth you "pressing through" in order to maintain your joy, your sanity and your peace in the midst of frustrations. Some days you will sail on Cloud 9; other days it will be difficult just for you to put one foot in front of the other. However know that you can make it if you resolve to press on. *I press toward the mark for the prize of the high calling of God in Christ Jesus* (Philippians 3:14).

Faith – To know that with God on your side, the odds are never against you but always in your favor. *Now faith is the substance of things hoped for, the evidence of things not seen* (Hebrews 11:1).

Prayer – As I said in my book *25 Workplace Survival Tips for the Believer*, you must "pray to stay." Pray to stay set apart, sane, encouraged, faithful, hopeful and joyful. *Men ought always to pray and not faint* (Luke 18:1).

BIBLIOGRAPHY

Davis, Linsey & Hanan Karar. "Single, Black, Female—and Plenty of Company." *Abcnews.go.com,* 14 Dec. 2014. Web. 01 Jan. 2015.

Jones, Debby and Jackie Kendall. *Lady In Waiting: Developing Your Love Relationships.* Treasure House, Shippensburg, PA, 1995.

O'Neil, Tyler. "5 Bible verses to comfort struggling singles." *Christianpost.com.* 09 Nov. 2013. Web. 21 Oct. 2014

Smith, Lori. "Single Truths for Single Christians." *Lifeway.com.* 24 10 2014.

Zimmerman, Janet Ong. "What are you Worth?" *loveforsuccessfulwomen.com.* 1 Feb. 2012. Web. 24 10 2014.

To contact the author, please write:

DSB Life Solutions, LLC
P.O. Box 1877
Memphis, TN 38101

Website: www.demetriasbanks.com
Email: office@demetriasbanks.com

Other books by Demetria Springfield Banks:

Books:
- *25 Workplace Survival Tips for the Believer*
- *Prayer Pearls: Priceless Inspiration*
- *Healmotions: Unwrapping the Mummy Layers*
- *I Am Somebody That's Who I Am*
- *Surviving This Place: 20 Prayers for the Workplace*
- *Between the Watch, the Wait and God's Work*

Life Coaching Products:
LifeTrac Survival Tool Kit
Counter Clockwise: Taking It Back – The 3R's of Making a Comeback